# Penny
## The Forgotten Coin

To: Kyle,
Every
Penny
counts!

Denise Brennan-Nelson
2005

**By Denise Brennan-Nelson**

**Illustrated by Michael Glenn Monroe**

Sleeping Bear Press

*To Martin, Jane, John, Joey and Ryan*
*"I call heads!"*
*With love,*
—Denise


*To Heather and all the staff at Sleeping Bear Press.*
*Thank you for your hard work and commitment*
*to getting my books to people who love to read.*
—Michael

The American Red Cross name and emblem are copyrights of the American Red Cross. Used with permission.

Text Copyright © 2003 Denise Brennan-Nelson
Illustrations Copyright © 2003 Michael Glenn Monroe

Sleeping Bear Press
310 North Main Street, Suite 300
Chelsea, MI 48118
www.sleepingbearpress.com

Sleeping Bear Press is an imprint of The Gale Group, Inc.,
a division of Thomson Learning, Inc.

Printed and bound in Canada.

10 9 8 7 6 5 4 3 2 1

Library of Congress Cataloging-in-Publication Data
Brennan-Nelson, Denise.
Penny : the forgotten coin / by Denise Brennan-Nelson ; illustrated by Michael Glenn Monroe.
p. cm.
Summary: A penny begins to feel useless because her monetary value is small, but she remembers her history and feels proud when she is used to flip a coin.
ISBN 1-58536-128-3
1. Cent-Juvenile literature. [1. Cent. 2. Coins.] I. Monroe, Michael Glenn, ill. II. Title.
CJ1836 .B74 2003
737.4973—dc21
2003010462

## Author's Note:

**W**hen I was a kid I loved pennies! I loved the feel of them, their coppery color and the plinking sound they made when I dropped them into my piggy bank.

Pennies were special. They bought me bubblegum and wild horse rides. I grew up hearing "A penny saved is a penny earned," and my dad always told me, "Watch the pennies and the dollars will take care of themselves." Some of my favorite relatives were "penny-pinchers" and others were "penny-wise but pound-foolish."

Pennies were important. We used pennies to make wishes, bring us luck, and if we wanted to know what someone was thinking we would say, "A penny for your thoughts..."

As I got older I forgot how special pennies were, and one day (I'm ashamed to admit) I threw a penny away. It sat in my wastebasket for a few seconds before I picked it up out of the coffee grounds and banana peels. (I think I heard a little voice say, "Thank you.")

At that moment I sat down and started writing this story.

A penny can't buy what it did in the past. However, there is still a lot a penny can do. I have learned that many charities rely on the donation of pennies to help buy food, clothing, medical aid, and even teddy bears.

Writing this story made me realize that we are a little bit like pennies. "Everybody counts," and in some small way we can make a difference. So save your pennies and remember: Pennies are very special and important... JUST LIKE YOU!

*A child has a simple measure;*
*what lifts his heart becomes his treasure.*
*Heart-shaped rocks, a bouncy ball...*
*a feather on the ground.*
*Treasures sweet and simple*
*like a lucky penny found.*

With special thanks to the Livingston County Chapter of the American Red Cross.

—Denise Brennan-Nelson

John and Joey raced to the end of the driveway.
As they stopped to turn their bikes around,
the glint of something shiny caught John's eye.

"Hey look!" John said. "There's a penny!"

"Big deal!" Joey said.

"Dad says you can't do anything with a penny these days."

John bent down and plucked the penny from the dirt.
Turning it over to admire both sides, he whispered to himself,

*"Find a penny, pick it up;*
*all day long, have good luck."*

Deciding that the penny belonged with his other treasures,
John dropped it into his pocket.

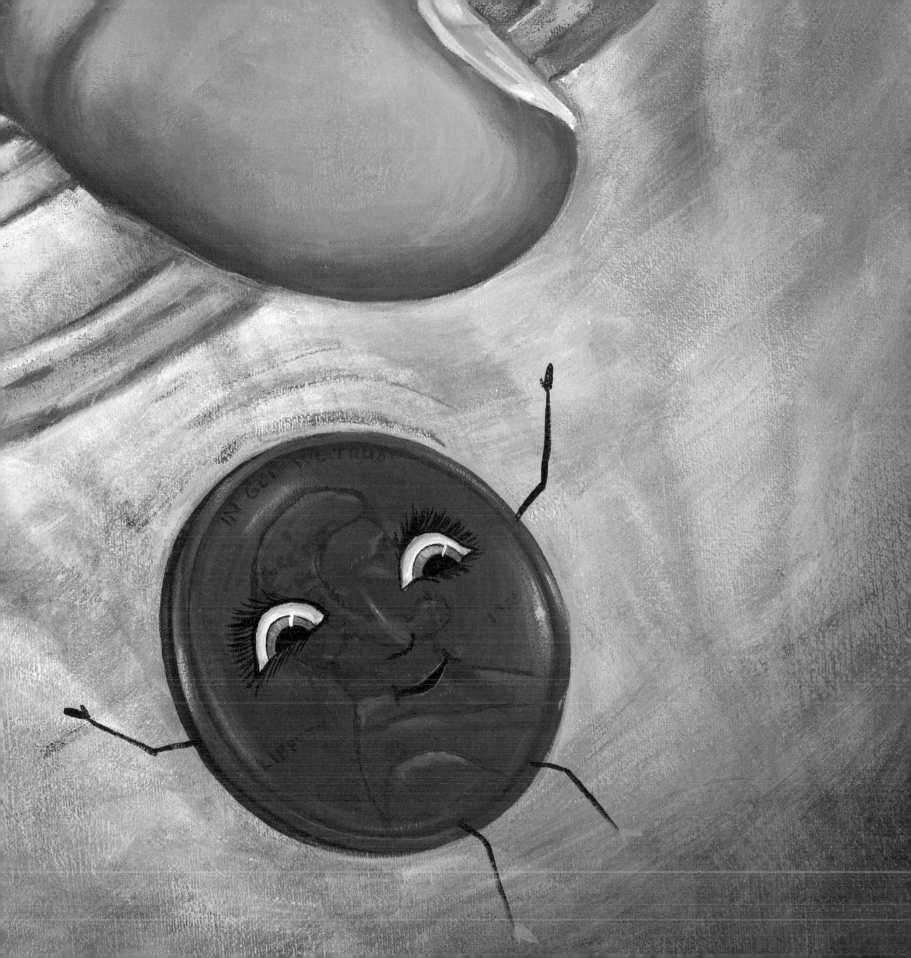

Penny slowly opened her eyes. Looking around she saw Marble, Rock, Super Ball, Feather, String, and Bubblegum. They all began talking at once!

"What do you want?"
Rock grumbled.

"Why are you here?"
Marble demanded.
"What can you do?"
snapped Super Ball.

Bubblegum sneered, "She can't do anything.
She can't even buy ME anymore!"
Before Penny could tell them what John had said,
the treasures began chanting:

"Penny, Penny what a bore! Can't do anything anymore."

Humiliated, Penny sank to the bottom of the grimy pocket.
Looking up at the treasures she thought, "Maybe they're right."

Marble was beautiful, so smooth and round.
And Feather's bold, vibrant colors made it easy
to see why John had kept him.
Rock had shimmering speckles and sharp, ragged edges,
and John could blow bubbles as big as balloons with Bubble Gum.
Penny knew the boys would have hours of fun bouncing Super Ball
in the driveway. And John needed String—without it, he couldn't fly his kite.

Feeling lonely and sad,
Penny curled up in the bottom
of John's pocket and wondered,
"Who needs me? What can I do?"

The first one-cent coin was created in 1787. It was called the Fugio cent and was 100% copper. Paul Revere supplied some of the copper used for these coins. Since then there have been 11 different designs for our one-cent coin. Currently the penny is made of 97.6% zinc and 2.4% copper.

If you have a nickname, you have something in common with the penny. "Penny" comes from the British coin "pence" and is only a nickname for our one-cent copper coin.

Pennies and other coins are made at mints. The first mint was established in 1792. The United States has four mints. They are located in Washington D.C.; Philadelphia, Pennsylvania; Denver, Colorado; and West Point, New York. Pennies are made at the Denver and Philadelphia mints only. If you look closely at a penny you will see a "D" or a "P." This tells you which mint produced that penny.

More pennies are made than any other coin. There were 7,288,855,000 pennies made in 2002! How long would it take to roll that many pennies? How many dollars would you have?

A penny saved is a penny earned.

¢

The penny appears in many of our everyday expressions such as "Penny-wise and pound-foolish," "A penny saved is a penny earned," and "A penny for your thoughts." How many thoughts would you give for a penny?

Abraham Lincoln first appeared on the penny in 1909, the 100th anniversary of his birth. He was the first president to appear on an American coin. Some people thought that someone as important as Lincoln deserved to be on a higher denomination than the penny. Others thought that because Lincoln was known as the "common people's president," he was the right person.

The Lincoln Memorial was added to the back of the penny to mark Lincoln's 150th birthday. Do you know what year that was? The penny is the first and only coin to have the same person on both sides. Look very closely at the Lincoln Memorial on the back of the penny. What do you see? The statue of Lincoln is inside the memorial.

# ...being clutched in Rebecca's hand, and her smile at the candy store.

 It's hard to believe but in the 1930s and 1940s you could buy candy with one penny! My mom and dad have told me stories about going to the local store and buying a piece of fudge and other yummy treats for just one cent each.

Ask your grandpa and grandma what they bought with a penny. They might also remember the steel pennies that were made in 1943. Because of the war there was a copper shortage so they made zinc-coated steel pennies. I have one that my dad gave me! It looks funny and is lighter than a copper penny.

She remembered the fountain
and the secret wishes...

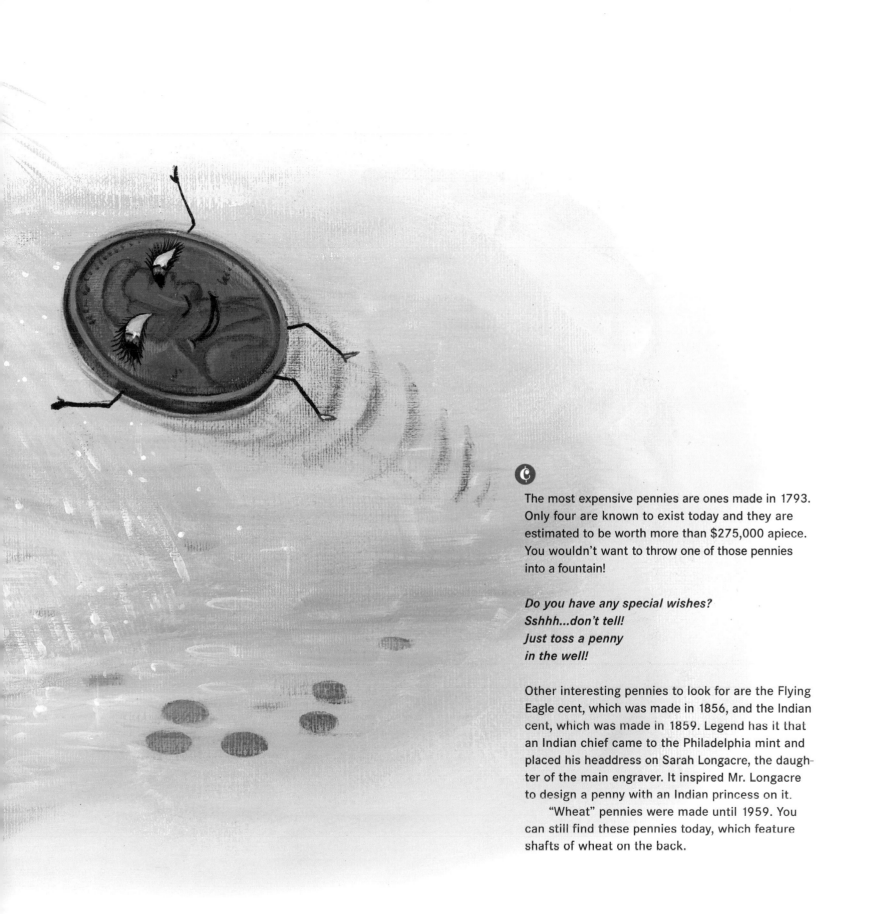

The most expensive pennies are ones made in 1793. Only four are known to exist today and they are estimated to be worth more than $275,000 apiece. You wouldn't want to throw one of those pennies into a fountain!

*Do you have any special wishes?*
*Sshhh...don't tell!*
*Just toss a penny*
*in the well!*

Other interesting pennies to look for are the Flying Eagle cent, which was made in 1856, and the Indian cent, which was made in 1859. Legend has it that an Indian chief came to the Philadelphia mint and placed his headdress on Sarah Longacre, the daughter of the main engraver. It inspired Mr. Longacre to design a penny with an Indian princess on it.

"Wheat" pennies were made until 1959. You can still find these pennies today, which feature shafts of wheat on the back.

# ...and being scooped up from penny dishes.

 Have you ever noticed which way Abraham Lincoln is facing on the penny? If you said "right," you are correct! All other portraits of presidents on U.S. coins face to the left. David Brenner designed the Lincoln penny using a photograph that was taken of Abraham Lincoln on February 9, 1864. In the photograph, Lincoln is facing to the right.

Have you ever wondered why the head side of a coin and the tail side are upside down from each other? This is called a "coin turn." There is no particular reason why the mint makes the coins this way.

## She had visited some funny and unusual places...

¢

In 1936 the G.H. Bass Shoe Company introduced the penny loafer. They became popular very quickly! It was originally called the Bass Weejun (short for Norwegian). The penny loafer is a leather slip-on with a half pocket on the front of the shoe. You could slip a penny into the pocket on the front of the shoe for luck or to carry spare change. Do you know anyone who owned a pair of penny loafers? Ask your mom and dad if they wore penny loafers.

...but her favorite of all was watching the races!

Over the past couple of years there has been talk about getting rid of the penny. Some people think we don't need them. They have suggested that we round up or down to the nearest nickel. What do you think? I like pennies! They're different, and the penny is our country's oldest coin.

For now, at least, there is no plan of discontinuing the production of pennies. The penny is very profitable for our treasury. Each penny costs eight-tenths of a cent to make. The profit on the penny was more than $24 million last year! (Wow!)

## She hummed her song and it seemed to Penny...

♩

In 1936 Bing Crosby recorded a song called *Pennies from Heaven* with the Jimmy Dorsey Orchestra. It was featured in a movie of the same name, and the song won an Oscar. It is a beautiful song that tells us storms were made to help us appreciate blue skies and sunny days. When it rains, turn your umbrella upside down to catch *Pennies from Heaven*.

# ...that her value was great and her uses were many!

We use telephones, faxes, and e-mails to communicate, but at one time, penny postcards were used. The penny postcard era was from 1898 to 1951. The stamp to mail a postcard during that time cost only a penny.

If you look very closely at a penny you will see some interesting things. Curving around the upper border of the penny are the words *United States of America*. Directly below that is our national motto: *E Pluribus Unum*, which means "one of many." Over Lincoln's portrait the words, "In God We Trust" are written, and first appeared on the penny in 1909.

In 1959, Mr. Frank Gasparro was selected to create a new design for the reverse of the penny. His initials appear on the penny to the right of the shrubbery.

"I'm not like the other treasures," Penny thought,

"I can't sparkle, fly or bounce....

...but I know I'm very special,

because every penny counts."

Penny's thoughts were interrupted by the sound of John and Joey's voices.

"I go first!" Joey shouted.

"No! I go first!" insisted John, then he suggested,

"Wait—let's flip a coin!"

The treasures looked at each other,
wondering what would happen next.

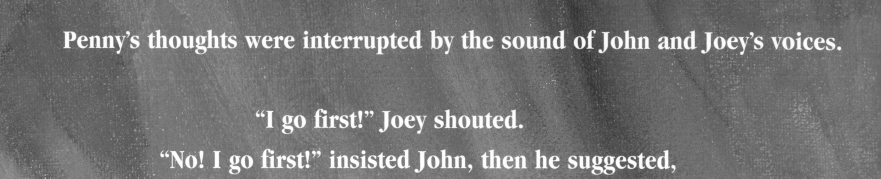

John's fingers fumbled around in his pocket until he found Penny.
As he lifted her up past the other treasures, they shouted,
"Where do you think you're going?"

Without hesitation, Penny smiled proudly and answered,
"John needs me!"

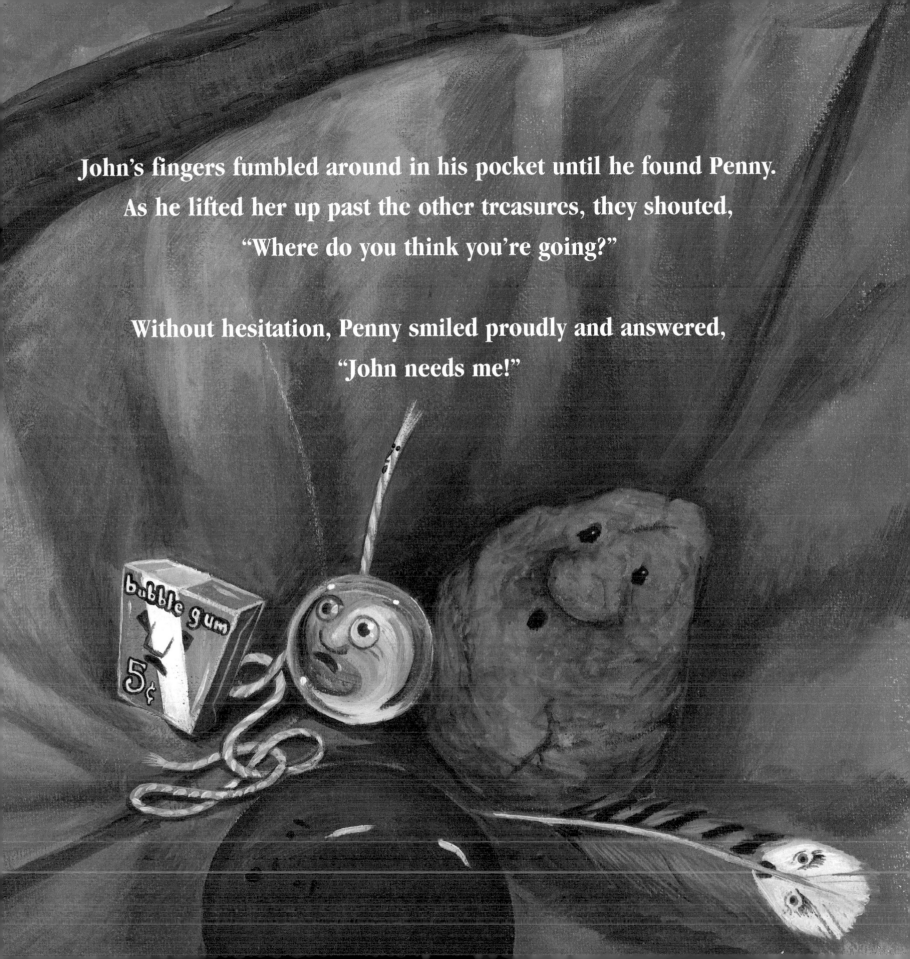

"I call heads!" John shouted,
tossing Penny into the air.

Whe he lifted his hand,
John smiled and whispered:

*"Find a penny, pick it up;*
*all day long, have good luck."*

When pennies come off the press they are very shiny. Over time they become tarnished. Tarnish on a coin is a chemical process caused by oxygen acting on the metal, or by chemicals that the coin comes in contact with. The most common chemical that causes tarnish is sulfur, which is found in most paper. Coin collectors wrap coins in a sulphur-free paper.

## Copper Magic

Pour vinegar into a jar and add a touch of salt. Put 10-15 pennies into the vinegar for at least five minutes. Clean an iron nail thoroughly with scouring powder, then rinse, making sure the powder is completely removed. Drop the nail into the jar along with the pennies and let them sit overnight.

## What happened?

The vinegar and salt dissolved the layer of tarnish from the surface of the pennies, leaving them shiny. The removing of the tarnish released copper ions into the vinegar. These ions then reacted with the iron in the nail, which formed copper metal and coated the surface of the nail.

**Denise Brennan-Nelson's** boundless energy and enthusiasm comes from her days as a motivational speaker. Since the publication of her first book, *Buzzy the bumblebee* in 1999, Denise has taken that enthusiasm into schools and inspired thousands of children to "bee-lieve" in themselves. She is also the author of *My Momma Likes to Say*, a humorous look at idioms and clichés and their origins.

Denise lives in Howell, Michigan, with her husband Bob and their two daughters, Rebecca and Rachel.

Award-winning wildlife artist **Michael Glenn Monroe** is known for his charming character illustrations in such titles as *Buzzy the bumblebee, A Wish to be a Christmas Tree*, and *The Christmas Humbugs*. He has also illustrated state alphabet titles from Sleeping Bear Press including *M is for Mitten: A Michigan Alphabet, S is for Sunshine: A Florida Alphabet*, and *L is for Last Frontier: An Alaska Alphabet*.

Michael lives in Brighton, Michigan, with his wife Colleen (author of *A Wish to Be a Christmas Tree* and *The Christmas Humbugs*) and their three children, twins Natalie and Matthew and son John.